A Really Good Scare

written by Danny Katz
illustrated by Mitch Vane

PEARSON
Education
Australia

WorldCom Edu

Desk Copy Request / Information

To place your desk copy request or for more information,
please contact the following office:
Tel : (02)3273-4300   Fax : (02)3273-4303

Contents

Welcome to *Magic Reader*

How to Use *Magic Reader*

Characters

Chapter One
The Bookworm   7

Chapter Two
In the Classroom   13

Chapter Three
At Lunchtime   19

Chapter Four
After School   27

Chapter Five
The New Boy   37

Exercises

Glossary

About the Author
and Illustrator

Welcome to Magic Reader

Character sketches provide prior information about the main characters

Repetitive and straightforward story lines

Predictable format

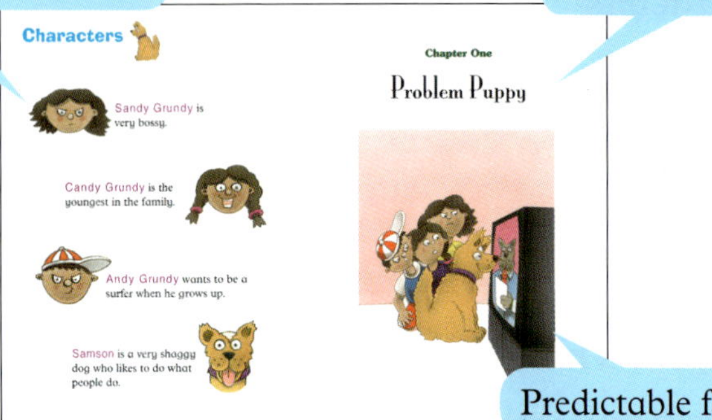

Familiar content related to everyday experiences

Full-color illustrations

Simply constructed sentences

A variety of simple sentence patterns

Includes oral and written language patterns

Use of high-frequency words

How to Use Magic Reader

Step 1. Listen to the Story

You'll love listening to the audio as you follow the flow of the story, even if you don't understand every single word or sentence.

Step 2. Read along with the Story

While improving your pronunciation and your ability to memorize sentences, you'll build confidence as you listen to and then read along with the audio in a loud voice.

Step 3. Listen to Specific Parts of Each Chapter

With each chapter broken up into sections, you'll be able to fully understand the meaning of each part as you listen.

Step 4. Try the Activity Questions

Make sure you fully understand the meaning of each story by doing the accompanying exercises.

Characters 

Smart Alec thinks she is smarter than all her friends.

Molly P. Crisp likes to paint.

Barney Gavarney likes to sit quietly to eat his lunch.

The **new boy** at school likes to do things his own way.

The Bookworm

Smart Alec liked to read books. She liked to read all kinds of books. She liked storybooks. She liked picture books. She liked funny books. She liked sad books.

Smart Alec liked books that were so big
and heavy that she had to ask the
Henson twins to hold the books up while
she read.

She liked reading every kind of book.
That's how Smart Alec got to be so
smart.

Smart Alec's favorite books were about animals. She loved reading about animals, especially animals that lived in the jungle.

One day Smart Alec went to the library,
as usual. She sat and read about big,
fierce lions. She read about huge, scary
tigers. And enormous, frightening rhinos.

Smart Alec wanted to know what the jungle animals looked like. And what they liked to eat. And what terrible, horrible, awful noises they liked to make. Then Smart Alec thought how wonderful it would be to be a big, scary animal.

Chapter Two

In the Classroom

Molly P. Crisp was sitting at her desk painting a picture. It was a picture of a lovely house with blue flowers out the front. Smart Alec spotted her from afar.

Smart Alec pretended to be a big, fierce lion. She started to creep across the floor. Slowly, slowly she prowled. Slowly, slowly she stalked.

She kept her body close to the ground and used her lion ears to listen for sounds.

She got closer and closer, creeping under tables, slinking around chairs, crawling over backpacks and books. Smart Alec crept right up to Molly P. Crisp. Then she leapt up and screamed at the top of her lungs, "ROARRRRRRRRRR!"

Molly P. Crisp got such a fright, she threw her hands in the air and accidentally painted a big, blue line on her face.

"I'm a big, fierce lion and I live in the jungle!" said Smart Alec. "I am the King of the Beasts because I'm strong and powerful. And I have a terrrr-i-ble ROARRRRRRRRR!"

Smart Alec looked like she really did
believe she was a fierce lion. "I love to eat
deer and antelope and zebras," she roared.
"And I'm so hungry right now, that I could
even eat YOU!"

Molly P. Crisp jumped up and knocked over her bottle of paint. Paint spilt all over her desk. And ruined her beautiful picture.

Then Smart Alec strutted away proudly because she was a big, fierce lion in the jungle.

Chapter Three

MR-G3-25
MP3

At Lunchtime

Barney Gavarney was sitting on a bench in the playground, eating his lunch.

He had a drink on his lap, an apple in one hand and a tasty piece of cheese in the other hand.

Smart Alec spotted Barney Gavarney and began circling around him from far away. Now she was a huge, scary tiger. Quickly, quickly she ran. Quickly, quickly she sprinted.

She used her tiger muscles to leap and her tiger eyes to look this way and that.

She got closer and closer, springing
over bushes, darting around trees,
hurdling over sticks and stones and sand.
Smart Alec bounded right up to Barney
Gavarney.

Then she pounced and screamed at the
top of her lungs, "GROWLLLLLLLLL!"

Barney Gavarney got such a fright, he threw his cheese into the air. It bounced off his head and rolled behind the slide.

"I'm a huge, scary tiger and I live in the jungle!" said Smart Alec. "I am the largest member of the cat family. I'm famous for my black stripes, my amazing speed and my horrrr-i-ble GROWLLLLLLLL!"

"I can swim across rivers and I can climb to the treetops. But most of all I love to eat! I love to eat toads and tortoises and wild pigs. And I'm so hungry at the moment, that I may even eat YOU!"

Barney Gavarney jumped up and spilt his juice all over the place. It went all over his shirt and all over his shoes. It went all down his leg, which was really gross because juice is really sticky.

Then Smart Alec bounded away quickly because she was a huge, scary tiger that lived in the jungle.

Chapter Four

After School

It was the end of the day and Smart Alec was heading home. She was walking across the playground when she noticed a boy walking ahead of her. He was the new boy in her class. He'd just started school this week.

Smart Alec barely even knew his name.

And he didn't really know Smart Alec.

But Smart Alec still thought it would be

fun to give him a really good scare.

She pretended she was an enormous, frightening rhinoceros. She began snorting. She began stamping her feet.

29

Then Smart Alec marched toward the new boy. She used her heavy weight to push herself forward and her rhinoceros nose to sniff him out.

She stomped closer and closer, trampling over grass, stamping over twigs, stomping over dust and dirt and mud. Smart Alec came right up to the new boy and charged at him.

She screamed at the top of her lungs, "YARGHHHHHHHHH!"

The new boy didn't run away. He didn't
even move. He just turned around and
looked at her. Smart Alec was a little
surprised. She didn't know what to do.

"I'm an enormous, frightening rhinoceros and I live in the jungle!" she said. "I'm one of the largest animals on Earth and I'm even heavier than a car. I have a horn on the front of my head that is very dangerous. And I'm so hungry, that I think I'm going to eat YOU!"

The new boy wasn't even a little bit
scared. He just stood there quietly. Then
he cleared his throat. "The rhinoceros is
actually a peaceful animal," the new boy
said. "The rhinoceros does not attack
unless he has to defend himself."

"And the horn on the front of his head is not dangerous. In fact, it's made out of the same stuff your fingernails are made of, so it's very soft and delicate."

"And a rhinoceros would NEVER eat
me. The rhinoceros only eats plants.
They eat leaves and seedlings and small
bushes."

Chapter Five

The New Boy

Smart Alec was in shock. She tried to make a rhinoceros noise, but nothing would come out. She tried to stamp her rhinoceros feet, but they just wouldn't stomp. She tried to stare at the new boy with her rhinoceros eyes, but the new boy just stared back.

Then the new boy said, "I'm a giant, terrifying crocodile and I live in the jungle. I am one of the largest reptiles on Earth and I have a long, powerful tail for swimming."

Smart Alec thought the new boy really
believed he was a terrifying crocodile.

The new boy said, "I like to eat fish
and birds and small mammals and I'm
so hungry, I could gobble you up with
one big SNAPPPPPPPPP."

Smart Alec got such a fright, she ran all
the way home.

The new boy's name was Brainy
Delaney and he liked to read a lot of
books, too.

EXERCISES

Name _______________________

Retelling the story

Draw pictures and write captions to retell the story of
A Really Good Scare.

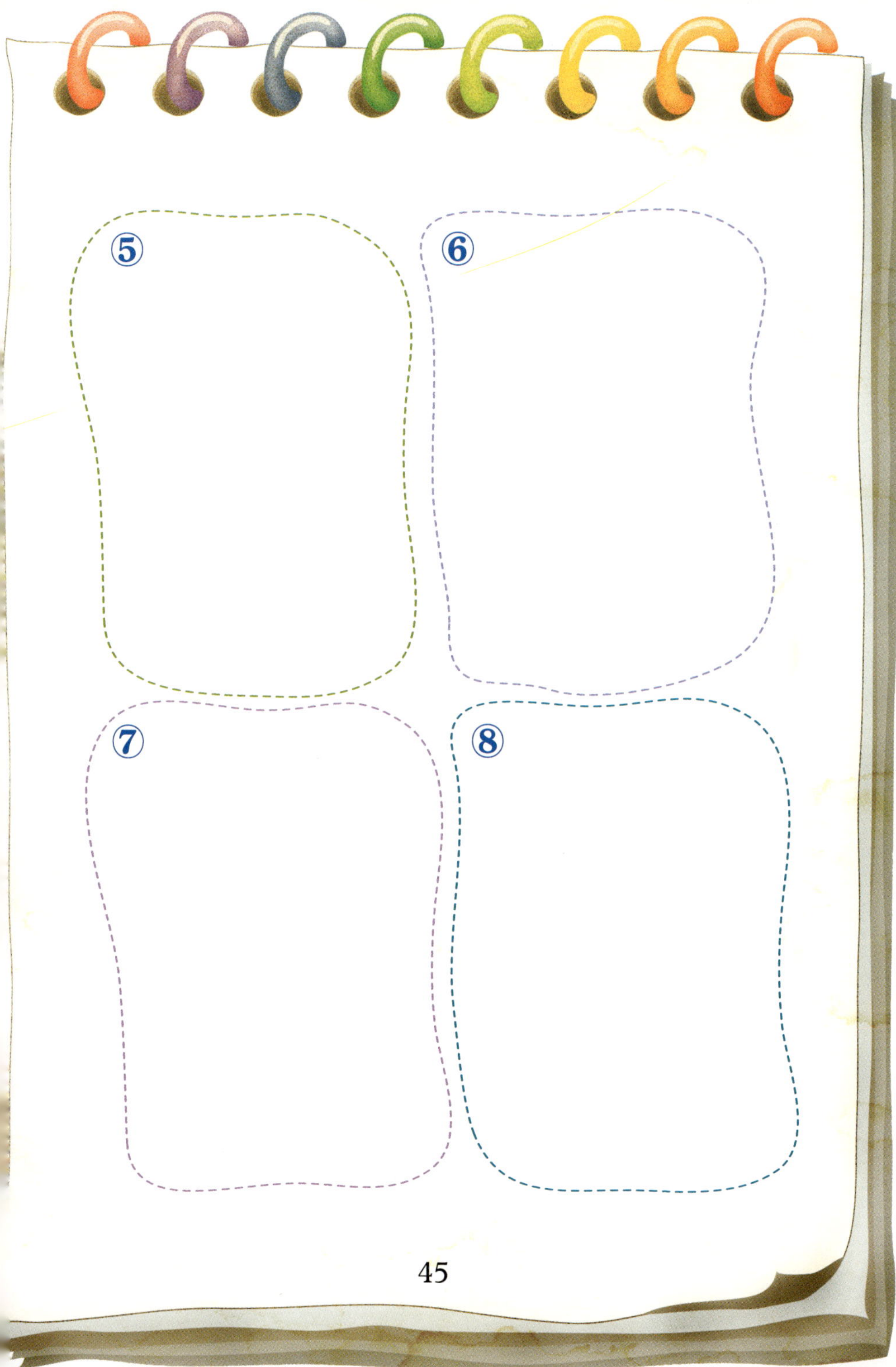
⑤
⑥
⑦
⑧

Animal descriptions

Write descriptions of these animals using some of the describing words given. You might like to add some describing words of your own.

elephant (big, huge, enormous, long, gray, wrinkly, tiny, rough, powerful)

____

____

____

____

giraffe (tall, long, thin, curved, patterned, sleek, large, slow, peaceful)

____

____

____

____

koala (small, furry, gray, soft, cuddly, sharp, bright, sleepy)

____

____

____

____

____

your pet or a friend's pet

____

____

____

____

____

____

Letter clusters

Below are some of the initial word blends from the book A Really Good Scare. Read the examples below for each of these initial blends: "st", "fr", "pr" and "cr". Now hunt for some other words that have these initial blends and add these to your list. You may need to look in dictionaries, books and print around the classroom.

st	fr	pr	cr
sticks	fright	prowled	crept
stones	frightened	proudly	creeping
stamping	front	pretended	crawling
stomped			

If there is time, use some of there words to write your own sentences.

____

____

____

____

____

____

____

____

____

____

Glossary

twins `n.` siblings born at the same time

Smart Alec liked books that were so big and heavy that she had to ask the Henson twins to hold the books up while she read.

jungle `n.` a wild land crowded with thick plants and trees, located in very hot climates

She loved reading about animals, especially animals that live in the jungle.

fierce `adj.` wild, violent

She sat and read about big, fierce lions.

spot (-spotted) `v.` to see, to find by seeing

Smart Alec spotted her from afar.

creep (-crept) `v.` to move slowly close to the ground, to prowl

She started to creep across the floor.

stalk (-stalked) `v.` to secretly follow

Slowly, slowly she stalked.

accidentally `adv.` doing something that you did not want to do

Molly P. Crisp got such a fright, she threw her hands in the air and accidentally painted a big, blue line on her face.

lungs `n.` the part of the body that breathes air

Then she leapt up and screamed at the top of her lungs.

Glossary

ruin (-ruined) `v.` to destroy, to mess up

And ruined her beautiful picture.

hurdle (-hurdled) `v.` to jump over

She got closer and closer, springing over bushes, darting around trees, hurdling over sticks and stones and sand.

pounce (-pounced) `v.` to attack by jumping on someone or something

Then she pounced and screamed at the top of her lungs, "GROWLLLLLLLLL!"

gross `adj.` very bad or unpleasant

It went all down his leg, which was really gross because juice is really sticky.

barely `adv.` hardly, almost not, only just

Smart Alec barely even knew his name.

snort (-snorted) `v.` to breathe with a very loud, harsh sound

She began snorting.

gobble (-gobbled) `v.` to eat quickly and swallow

"I like to eat fish and birds and small mammals and I'm so hungry, I could gobble you up with one big SNAPPPPPPPPP."

Author: Danny Katz

Danny Katz writes for the *Age*, *Good Weekend*, and the *West Australian*. He is the author of the bestselling humor book, *Spit the Dummy*, and has also written several kids' books — not to mention, he says, a big-budget Broadway musical that nobody seems terribly interested in producing.

Illustrator: Mitch Vane

Mitch Vane has been working as a freelance illustrator for twenty years. Her work includes cartoons, book covers, advertising, and editorial illustrations, but most of her work is in children's book illustrations. Her cartoons appear weekly in the *Age*.